SCOTTISH EPITAPHS

Raymond Lamont-Brown

Chambers

Published 1990 by W & R Chambers Ltd,
43-45 Annandale Street, Edinburgh EH7 4AZ

British Library Cataloguing in Publication Data
Lamont-Brown, Raymond
    Scottish Epitaphs
    1. Scotland. Graveyards. Monumental
    inscriptions: Epitaphs
    I. Title
    929.5'09411

ISBN 0-550-20058-4

Illustrations by John Haxby
Cover design by John Marshall

Typeset by Bookworm Typesetting Ltd, Edinburgh
Printed in Singapore by
Singapore National Printers Ltd

Contents

Preface

There was a time in Scotland when no man or woman, who thought they had amounted to anything, would dream of letting death creep up on them without first having immortalised themselves with an apt epitaph. Harlots, soldiers, clergymen, businessmen and crooks alike had one thing in common, apart from an acceptance of the inevitable – they all had an epitaph. Nowadays large sums of money are lavished on a funeral, and expensive coffins are an arguable expression of worldly wealth and prosperity that is only seen but once. Our ancestors had a better sense of graveyard values and lavished money on fine epitaphs which they believed would last forever.

Epitaphs developed in Scotland out of the fashions relating to tombstones. First there were the symbol stones of pagan times which continued till the Christian era to evolve as the headstones we know today. Although the Pope, St Gregory I, called 'the Great' (590–604) authorised relatives to erect tablets with epitaphs on graves (for prayers for the welfare of the souls of the dead), graveyards for the ordinary man and woman did not appear until the eleventh century and commemorative stones appeared much later. It was the Anglo-Normans who brought the recumbent effigy tombs to Scotland and these were very popular until the thirteenth century. These tombs with their simple Latin epitaphs tell us a lot about the fashions and customs of the time.

Epitaphs of medieval times mirror the early Christian ones in that they were usually in the form of tender prayers both for the living and the dead, whereas those of the Elizabethan and Jacobean eras were more often historical and stated who a person was and what he or she did. From 1600 to c.1650 epitaphs were poetic, changing to inscriptions of one line or phrase under Cromwell's rule, but during the period 1660 to 1680 they became long-winded. As a rule the most humorous of the epitaphs extant today in Scotland date from 1700 to around 1760, and from this period we still have a great variety of the work of local rhymesters. Many a village minister or parish dominie, as this collection shows, had a stab at the epitaph and their work is seen from Wick to Wigtown.

That is broadly how epitaphs began in Scotland, but where can they be found? It is not a platitude to say that the richest source of epitaphs is the burial ground, for epitaphs seem to crop up in the most unlikely places. The oldest epitaphs are mainly to be found at the south side of a pre-Reformation church, as people wished to avoid the shadow of the church falling on their graves. This was considered very unlucky, and the north also was associated with the devil – that is the main reason why suicides were buried in the north of a churchyard in pre-Reformation times to act as a first line of defence against the devil. Superstition may be cited too as the explanation why churchyards are often higher on the south side than the north, or higher than the road outside the church door-sill; for it was the medieval custom to bury the dead on top of others, and so gradually the ground became elevated.

Apart from the town and graveyards, other places to look for epitaphs include castle cemeteries and fort burial grounds. Because of the Reformation, epitaphs are far travelled; when the brave Reformers destroyed the abbeys and churches of the medieval church they often made quarries out of the ruins, and from the church pavements they removed tomb slabs for use in the construction of their own houses and barns. So it is not unsual to find the tomb slab with the epitaph of a senior clergyman now as a door-lintel, a fireplace or a window slab. A good example of this is to be found at Queen Mary's house in North Street, St Andrews, where there is the re-used tombstone of Archdeacon Inglis, who died c.1411, from the nearby ruined cathedral.

Fundamentally, the aim of the epitaph is to give details of the person buried below, but there is more to it than that. For throughout the centuries Scottish epitaphs have provided a fascinating insight into the rural and social history of their time. Today epitaphs in Scottish town and country churchyards show as well as any verse the many emotions of man, so that any handful of epitaphs is a collation of tears and laughter, wisdom grave and light wit, fear and courage. Epitaphs fit every mood. Quite often epitaphs are all that is left to us of a local ballad or folk rhyme; they are no less important for telling us something about local people, who they were, what they did and what standing they had in their communities.

GRAVE NEWS
FROM SCOTLAND

In the graveyards of Scotland then, the moving finger of time was halted long enough to print, often in splendid Gothic script, a unique collection of interesting statements. For nothing concentrated the literary mind bent on gossip and invective more than the thought of having to sum up in just a few words a whole lifetime of theft, hypocrisy, generosity and endeavour. Witty, vicious, accusing, romantic and downright tragic, all sentiments are to be found enshrined forever (allowing for vandals social and civic) in the graveyards of Scotland.

Reading epitaphs is rather like perusing someone's most intimate diaries. Just as most diaries are not published until the author has passed hence, to avoid embarrassment, the epitaph was used to say things one would not have dreamed of saying in life. Witness this on the tomb of a violinist from the *Mearns*:

> When Orpheus played he moved Old Nick,
> But when you played you made us sick.

Scotland is rich in such epilaughs:

The Talkative Maid of Dalry

Beneath this silent tomb is laid
A noisy antiquated maid,
Who from her cradle talked till death
And ne'er before was out of breath.

Unlucky Calton Man

Here lies the body of William Beck
He was thrown at a hunt and broke his neck.

Glasgow's Sullen Story

Here lies John Sullen, and it is God's will
He that was sullen should be sullen still;
He still is sullen, if the truth ye seek;
Knock until Domesday, Sullen will not speak.

Greedy Tam Reid of Cromarty

Here lies Tam Reid
Who was chokit to deid
Wi' takin a feed
O' butter and breed
Wi' owre muckle speed,
When he had nae need,
But just for greed.

owre muckle, excessive

Scottish Wisdom from Coatbridge

Here lies the body of Georgie Denham
If ye saw him now ye wadna ken him.

From the Churchyard, Aberdeen

Here lie the bones of Elizabeth Charlotte,
Born a virgin, died a harlot.
She was aye a virgin at seventeen,
A remarkable thing in Aberdeen.

From a Churchyard near Greenock
Roger's Razor Slipped

Here lies, alas! poor Roger Norton,
Whose sudden death was oddly brought on!
Trying one day his corns to mow off,
The razor slipped and cut his toe off!
The toe, or rather what it grew to,
The part then took to mortifying.
Which was the cause of Roger's dying.

Letitia the Sailor's Daughter from Granton

Grim death, to please his liquorish palate
Has taken my Lettice to put in his sallat.

Mr Knott from Perth

Here lies a man who was Knott born;
His father was Knott before him.
He lived Knott, and he did Knott die,
Yet underneath this stone doth lie.

> Knott christened,
> Knott begot.
> And here lies,
> And yet was Knott.

*At Reid Churchyard in the Parish of Gairtney,
Annandale*

I, Jocky Bell o' Brakenbrow, lyes under this stane,
Five of my awn sons laid it on my wame;
I liv'd aw my days, but sturt or strife
Was man o' my meat, and maister o' my wife;
If you've done better in your time than I
    did in mine
Take the stane aff my wame, and lay it on thine.

wame, stomach; *sturt*, trouble

John Sim of Peterhead

Wha lies here?
John Sim, ye needna' speir.
Hullo, John, is that you?
Ay, ay, but I'm deid noo.

speir, inquire

In Forfar Churchyard

'Tis here that Tibby Allan lies,
'Tis here, or here about,
But no one till the Resurrection day,
Shall the very spot dispute.

On Mr Strange

This is perhaps one of Scotland's most popular epitaphs for it occurs in several churchyards:

Here lies an honest lawyer —
That is Strange!

Using, of course, a pun on the word and name Strange.

The Noble Laird

Here lies the Laird O' Lundie
Sic transit gloria mundi.

(i.e. 'Thus passes away the glory of this world.')

Aberdeen

Here lies Martin Elginbrod,
Have mercy on my soul, Lord God,
As I would do were I Lord God,
And Thou were Martin Elginbrod.

Deer, Aberdeenshire

Here lies an old woman wrapt in her linen,
Mother to James and Thomas Binnen;
Who for want of a coffin was buried in a girnal,
The earth got the shell, and the De'il got the kernel.

girnal, meal-chest

4

Cullen Graveyard, Banffshire

Here lies interred a man o' micht,
His name was Malcolm Downie:
He lost his life ae market nicht
By fa'in aff his pownie.

                    Aged 37 years

The Tall Man from Dumfries

Here lies Andrew MacPherson,
Who was a peculiar person;
He stood six foot two
Without his shoe,
And he was slew,
At Waterloo.

The Price of Prayer

Here lyeth the Body of DANIEL JEFFREY
He was buried ye 22 day of September 1746, in ye 18th
year of his age.

And from his tombstone which was once to be found in
Calder:

This youth, when in his sickness lay,
Did for the Minister send, that he would
Come and With him Pray, But he would not
                                        atend [sic],
But when this young man Buried was
The Minister did him admit he should be
Carried into Church, that he might money get.
By this you see what man will do to get
Money if he can, who did refuse to come
And pray by the foresaid young man.

An Auntie from Crail, Fife

Here lies my good and gracious Auntie,
Wham Death has packed in his portmanty,
Threescore and ten years did God gift her,
And here she lies, wha de'il daurs lift her?

5

From Newtyle Churchyard, Ruthven, Perthshire
A Sensible Man

Here lies the body of Robert Small,
Who, when in life, was thick not tall;
But what's of greater consequence
He was endowed with good sense.

In Durness Churchyard, Sutherland

Here doth lye the bodie
Of John Flye, who did die
By a stroke from a sky-rocket,
Which hit him in the eye-socket.

The Cattle Dealer from Kirkmichael

Here lies the body of Glencorse,
He went to the Borders with two horse,
He was a sheep and cattle-dealer,
At last gave up for want of siller.

siller, money

Greyfriars Kirkyard, Edinburgh

Here lies John and his Wife
Janet MacFee
40 hee – 30 shee

A Dunfermline Lad

Johnnie Carnegie lais heir
Descendant of Adam and Eve
Gif ony can gang hicher
I'se willing gie him leve.

hicher, higher

From Colvend, Kirkcudbrightshire
The Man of Odd Shape

Erected by John Young, Jr. to the memory of John Young, his father, who departed this life on the 26th of May 1788, aged 37 years.

'Here lies a just and squareman'

Torryburn, Fife

In this churchyard lies Eppie Coutts,
Either here, or hereabouts:
But where it is, none can tell
Till Eppie rise and tell hersel'.

Football at Fenwick, Ayrshire
James White, 1685

This martyr was by Peter Ingles shot,
By birth a Tiger rather than a Scot,
Who that his monstrous extract might be seen,
Cut off my head and kicked it o'er the Green.
Thus was the head which was to wear a crown
A football made by a profane dragoon.

A Curious End at Canonbie

Here lyes Francis Armstrong,
Son of William Armstrong
In Glinger
Who died of the water, on the Lord's Day,
Nov. 1 1696
As he went from the Kirk after sermon. Aged 20.

Graveyard Strip at Colvend, Kirkcudbrightshire

Unveil thy bosom faithful tomb
Take this new treasure to thy trust,
And give these scared relics room,
Awhile to slumber in the dust.

7

The Lush from Staplegordon

'J G W Died 1693'

He had a strong judgment, quick imagination and
    retentive Memory.
He possessed the love and respect of all who
knew him
Then he sullied it all.
He died of drink.

A tale from Dundee

Here lies the banes o' Tammas Messer
Of tarry woo he was a dresser:
He had some faults and mony merits,
And died o' drinkin' ardent spirits.

St Andrews Cathedral Churchyard
On a Ship's Captain and his Wife

Here we lie in a horizontal position like a
Ship laid up, stripped of her sails and rigging.

Also from St Andrews

'In Memory of . . . who fell off the Step Rock
into the arms of Jesus'

Biggar
Chatty Lady

On a cold pillow lies her head
Yet it will rise again 'tis said;
So prudently reader how thy walk
For if she rise again she'll talk!

From Sweetheart Abbey, Dumfries

Here lyes Thomas Black, in hopes of heaven
Who departed this life in 1711.
I, Thomas-like
Sometimes did doubt,
Yet Christ I owned
Without dispute.
Black I was, but
Comely through his grace
I'm glorious now
For still I see his face.

Elspeth Pye

Here lye I, Elspeth Pye
Four and twenty bairns, gudeman and I.

Dunsyre

In a vault underneath
Lie several of the Saunderses
Late of this parish – particulars
The last day will disclose.
Amen.

Good Show!

Sir Charles Coote
Killed at Trim, 7 May 1642
England's honour, Scotland's wonder
Ireland's terror here lies under.

A Record at Pumpherston

'To Nicholas Martin died 1595 – Nicholas ye first
and Martin ye last,
Goodnight Nicholas'

(i.e., he was the last of his family.)

From Lochtyside

As I was riding alang the road,
Not kennin' whit was comin'
An auld grey bull a' hornie cam'
After me a runnin';
He wi' his horny heid struck me
He being sore offended
I from ma horse, was forced to fa'
And so, my days were ended.

Oakfield Chopper

The Lord saw good, I was lopping off wood
And down fell from the tree.
I met with a check and broke my neck,
And so death lopped off me.

To Daisy at Dingwall

Farewell, thou little blooming bud
Just bursting into flower.

Sorbie Soldier

Here lies removed from mundane scenes,
A major of the King's Marines,
Under arrest in narrow borders
He rises not till further orders.

To William Pepper of Fife

Tho' hot my name, yet mild my nature,
I bore goodwill to every creature,
I brewed good ale, and sold it too,
And unto each I gave his due.

The Lucker Locksmith

A zealous locksmith dy'd of late
And did arrive at heaven's gate,
He stood without and would not knock,
Because he meant to pick the lock.

The Falkirk Flirt

Here lies in peace secure
A lass inclined to mirth
Who by way of making sure
Took her paradise on earth.

Does any Reader Know?

In an October 1940 issue of *John O' London*'s magazine
the following epitaph was published. The sender did not
know the exact location, but said it was Scottish!

Here lies the mother of children seven,
Four on earth and three in heaven;
The three in heaven preferring rather
To die with mother than live with father.

The debtor of Glasgow Necropolis

From duns secure (if creditors should come),
For once a debtor may be found at home;
By death arrested, and in Jail here laid,
The first, the last, the only debt he paid.

From Strichen, Aberdeenshire

In hope to sing without a sob
    the anthem ever new,
I gladly bid the dusty glob
    and vain delights adieu.

Dialect from Kennay, East Aberdeenshire

It maiters-na whaure we lie doon
If we sleep in the hope of a glorious risen.

Backhanded compliment from Pitmedden

TUMULUS JACOBI SETONI PITMEDDENI
QUEM TEGIT HOC CESPES FUSTU
SETONUS HONORAS DIVITIAS LUXU
POSSE CARERE DOCET.

('The tomb of James Seton of Pitmedden
Seton, whom this turf covers,
Teaches that honour can exist without happiness
Riches without enjoyment.')

SCOTTISH POETS AND THE EPITAPH

Many Scottish poets have made an attempt at the epitaph, with varying degrees of success. One little-known poet who tried was John Campbell.

John Campbell, of Bonnington Cottage, near Edinburgh, was a character. Among his other gifts was a turn for poetry, which he exercised greatly to his own enjoyment. Eighteen years before his death, he composed his funeral letter in verse. A few days before his demise he called for it and ordered it to be printed, and after inscribing several copies with his own hand, he caused them to be sent to those who were to carry him to the grave. The singular document read as follows:

Sir –
Wi' me
Life's weary battle's ower at last,
The verge o' time I've fairly past
My ransomed spirit now at rest
    Frae worldly harm;
To you my only last request,
    In humblest form
Presents, that ye wad condescend,
As auld acquaintance and a friend
My funeral party to attend –
    My parting scene.
And see my earthy part consigned
    To its earth again.
To rest till the redemption come,
Shall raise the body from the tomb,
And lead the blood-washed sinner home
    To Heavenly place,
To spend eternity to come
    I' joy and peace.

The period fixed when it's intendit,
That men's concern wi' me be endit,
My son on the neist page has penn'd it,
    Baith time and place;
Now hoping that you will attend it,
    I wish you peace.

When John Campbell was asked why he had taken such a notion, his characteristic reply was: 'I'm like the piper o' Falkland, wha tuned his pipes before he de'ed, to let folk ken wha he was.'

Another was Gordon Fraser

Erected to the Memory of Gordon Fraser, who wrote poems and songs on Wigtown.

O bury me at Wigtown,
And o'er me raise a modest stane,
Tae tell the folks when I am gane,
The cauld mools wrap the banes o' ane
Wha wrote and sang o' Wigtown.

mools,earth

Sir Walter Scott (1771–1832) tried his hand at it for the grave of Tom Purdie, his favourite servant:

'Here lies one who might be trusted with untold gold But not with unmeasured whisky.'

Even Thomas Babington Macaulay, better known as Lord Macaulay (1800–59), turned out an epitaph or two. Here is his most famous Scottish one, 'A Jacobite's Epitaph':

To my true King I offer'd free from stain
Courage and faith; vain faith and courage vain.
For him I threw lands, honours, wealth, away
And one dear hope, that was more prized than they.
For him I languish'd in a foreign clime,
Grey-hair'd with sorrow in my manhood's prime;
Heard on Lavernia Scargill's whispering trees,
And pined by Arno for my lovelier Tees;
Beheld each night my home in fever'd sleep,
Each morning started from the dream to weep;
Till God, who saw me tried too sorely, gave
The resting place I ask'd, an early grave.
O Thou, whom chance leads to this nameless stone,
From that proud country which was once mine own,
By those white cliffs I never more must see.
By that dear language which I spake like thee,
Forget all feuds, and shed one English tear
O'er English dust. A broken heart lies here.

Head and shoulders above them all was Robert Burns, who wrote the most and perhaps the finest eighteenth-century portfolio of Scottish epitaphs. Here is the complete collection:

Epitaph for Robert Aitken

Robert Aitken (1739–1807), a prosperous and convivial lawyer of the town of Ayr, was a great admirer of Burns's poems after their meeting in 1783.

Know thou, O stranger to the fame
Of this much lov'd, much honoured name!
(For none that knew him need be told)
A warmer heart Death ne'er made cold.

Epitaph on my Ever-Honoured Father

William Burnes (1721–84), the Bard's father, is buried in the ruined kirkyard of Alloway, Ayrshire. This kirk was the setting of a powerful scene in Burns's poem *Tam o' Shanter*. In the last line of the second verse Burns inserted a 'Goldsmith line':

O ye whose cheek the tear of pity stains,
Dear with pious rev'rence and attend!
Here lies the loving Husband's dear remains,
The tender Father, and the gen'rous Friend.

The pitying Heart that felt for human Woe;
The Dauntless heart that fear'd no human Pride;
The Friend of Man, to vice alone a foe;
'For ev'n his failings lean'd to Virtue's side'.*

*Burns took the line 'For ev'n his failings lean'd to Virtue's side' from Oliver Goldsmith's (1728–74) 'The Deserted Village' and its description of the 'village preacher'.

Epitaph to Swearing Burton

Burton was a dandy whom Burns once met in Dumfries. It was Burton's habit to introduce the word 'Damn' in every sentence.

Here cursing, swearing Burton lies,
A buck, a beau, or 'Dem my eyes!'
Who in his life did little good,
And his last words were 'Dem my blood'.

Epitaph on John Bushby

John Bushby (died 1802) of Tinwald Downs was a Dumfries lawyer and County Sheriff-Clerk. Burns dined at his mansion around 1793–94.

Here lies John Bushby, honest man
Cheat him Devil, if you can.

Epitaph for a Suicide

The only surviving clue to the suicide's identity are the initials D------ C------.

Here lies in earth a root of Hell,
Set by the Diel's ain dibble;
This worthless body damn'd himself,
To save the Lord the trouble.

Epitaph of my Own Friend and my Father's Friend, William Muir of Tarbolton Mill

William Muir (died 1793) was a man with the proverbial heart of gold; it was he and his family who took Jean Armour into their care when she was pregnant for the second time by Burns. He owned 'Willie's Mill' at Tarbolton.

An honest man here lies at rest,
As e'er God with His image blest!
The friend of man, the friend of truth;
The friend of age, and guide of youth;
Few hearts like his, with virtue warm'd,
Few heads with knowledge so informed,
If there's another world, he lives in bliss;
If there is none, he made the best of this.

Epitaph for Jessy Lewars

Jessy Lewars (1778–1855), the youngest daughter of John Lewars, Supervisor of Excise at Dumfries, was the last of Burns's heroines. During the last six months of Burns's illness Jessy helped to nurse him, and he fancied himself in love with her. She lies buried in St Michael's Churchyard, Dumfries, not far from the grave of Burns. These lines were written by Burns while Jessy suffered from a slight indisposition. 'In case of the worst,' joked Burns, 'let me provide you with an epitaph.'

Say, sages, what's the charm on earth
Can turn Death's dart aside?
It is not purity and worth,
Else Jessy had not died.

17

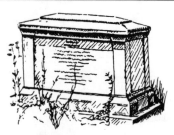

Epitaph on John Rankine

John Rankine (died 1810), a man of coarse good humour, farmed Adamhill, near Tarbolton. A friend of Burns in his Lochlea days.

Ae day, as Death, that gruesome carl,
Was driving to the tither warl'
A mixtie-maxtie motley squad,
And mony a guilt-bespotted lad;
Black gowns of each denomination,
And thieves of every rank and station,
From him that wears the star and garter,
To him that wintles in a halter:
Ashamed himself to see the wretches,
He mutters, glowrin' at the bitches,
'By God, I'll not be seen behint them,
Nor 'mang the sp'ritual core present them,
Without, at least, ae honest man,
To grace this damn'd infernal clan!'
By Adamhill a glance he threw,
'Lord God!' quoth he, 'I have it now,
There's just the man I want, i' faith!'
And quickly stoppit Rankine's breath.

wintles in a halter, waves to and fro hanging from a gallows

Epitaph on Captain Lascelles

Captain Edward Lascelles (1740–1820) was MP for Northallerton from 1761 to 1774 and entered the army on losing his seat. He regained his seat in 1790 and became 1st Earl of Harewood in 1812. The epitaph appears in the *Glenriddle Manuscripts* and Burns borrows his first line from Matthew Prior (1664–1721) 'when Bibo thought fit from this world to retreat'.

When Lascelles thought fit from this world to depart,
Some friends warmly thought of embalming his heart;
A bystander whispers – 'Pray don't make so much o' t,
The subject is poison, no reptile will touch it'.

Epitaph for a Lap Dog Named Echo

Written by Burns in 1793 to commemorate the death of
Mrs John Gordon's (later Viscountess Kenmure) pet.

In wood and wild, ye warbling throng,
Your heavy loss deplore!
Now half extinct your powers of song,
Sweet Echo is no more.

Ye jarring, screetching things around,
Scream your discordant joys!
Now half your din of tuneless sound
With Echo silent lies.

Extempore Epitaph

On a person nicknamed 'The Marquis', who asked Burns to
write an epitaph for him.
    'The Marquis' was a keeper of a respectable public house,
in Dumfries, and the alley in which the inn was situated was
called 'The Marquis's Close'.

Here lies a mock Marquis whose titles were shamm'd,
If ever he rise, it will be to be damned.

Epitaph for William Nicol

William Nicol (1744–97) became classics master in
the High School, Edinburgh in 1774. Burns became
a drinking crony of Nicol and the teacher accompanied
him on his tour of the Highlands.

Ye maggots, feed on Nicol's brain,
For few sic feasts you've gotten;
And fix your claws in Nicol's heart,
For deil a bit o' t's rotten.

Epitaph for Mr Ebenezer 'Willie' Michie, Schoolmaster of Cleish Parish, Fife

Ebenezer Michie (1766–1812) was schoolmaster first at Ker then at Cleish in Fife. Burns was introduced to him by Willian Nicol when they spent a boozy evening together. Michie fel asleep and Burns wrote an epitaph for him:

Here lie Willie Michie's banes,
O Satan! when ye tak' him,
Gie him the schulin' o' your weans,
For clever DEILS he'll mak' them!

Epitaph for William Cruickshank

William Cruickshank (died 1795) was appointed Rector of the High School, Canongate, Edinburgh in 1770. Later he became the Latin master at Edinburgh High School. Burns lodged with Cruickshank and his family at 2 St James's Square from the autumn of 1787 to 1788:

Honest Will to Heaven is gane,
And mony shall lament him;
His faults they a' in Latin lay,
In English nane e'er kent them.

Epitaph for John Dove

John Dove was the keeper of the Whiteford Arms, Mauchline. The Bachelors Club, of which Burns was a member, met at John Dove's inn.

Here lies Johnnie Pigeon;
What was his religion,
Whae'er desires to ken,
To some other warl',
Maun follow the carl,
For here Johnnie Pigeon had nane!

Strong ale was ablution,
Small beer persecution,
A dram was *memento mori*;
But a full-flowing bowl,
Was the saving of his soul,
And port was celestial glory.

Epitaph on a Henpecked Country Squire

In these three verses Burns was referring to William Campbell of Netherplace (died 1786), whose farm was next to Burns's property at Mossgiel. He was a man much ruled by his wife, Lilias Neilson (died 1826), daughter of a Glasgow merchant.

As father Adam first was fool'd,
(A case that's still too common,)
Here lies a man a woman ruled,
The Devil ruled the woman.

O Death, hads't thou but spar'd his life,
Whom we, this day, lament!
We freely wad exchanged the wife,
And a' been weel content.

E'en as he is, cauld in his graff,
The swap we yet will do 't;
Tak thou the carlin's carcase aff,
Thou'se get the saul o' boot.

And the nastiest verse:

One Queen Artemisia, as old stories tell,
When deprived of her husband she loved so well,
In respect for the love and affection he showed her,
She reduc'd him to dust and she drank up the powder.

But Queen Netherplace, of a diff'rent complexion,
When called on to order the fun'ral direction,
Would have eat her dead lord, on a slender pretence,
Not to show her respect, but – to save the expence!

Epitaph on Grizzel Grimme

A famous witch who lived at Lincluden in Kirkcudbrightshire, on the western outskirts of Dumfries, famous for its abbey and college, was given this epitaph:

Here lyes with Dethe auld Grizzel Grimme
Lincluden's ugly witche;
O Dethe, an' what a taste hast thou
Cann lye with sich a bitche!

Epitaph on Holy Wullie

'Holy Wullie' was William Fisher (1737–1809), a farmer at Montgarswood, Mauchline and elder of the kirk. It was he who pressed the Revd William 'Daddy' Auld (1709–91), the Mauchline minister, to take proceedings against those who did not attend church regularly. But Fisher, too, fell from grace on a charge of drunkenness.

Here Holy Wullie's sair-worn clay
Tak's up its last abode;
His saul has ta'en some other way,
I fear the left-hand road.

Stop! there he is as sure's a gun,
Poor, silly body, see him!
Nae wonder he's as black's the grun:
Observe wha's standing wi' him.

Your brunstane Devilship, I see,
Has got him there before ye;
But haud your nine-tail cat a wee,
Till ance you've heard my story.

Your pity I will not implore,
For pity ye have nane;
Justice, alas! has gi'en him o'er,
And mercy's day is gane.

But hear me, Sir, Diel as ye are,
Look something to your credit,
A coof like him wad stain your name
If it were kent ye did it.

coof, fool

Epitaph on a Noisy Polemic

The 'polemic' was James Humphrey (1755-1844), a mason from Mauchline.

Below thir stanes lie Jamie's banes'
O Death, it's my opinion,
Thou ne'er took such a bleth'ran bitch
Into thy dark dominion!

Inscription for the Headstone of Fergusson the Poet

Here lies Robert Fergusson
Born September 5th, 1751. Died October 16th, 1774.

In 1787, Burns commissioned an architect to erect a stone on Fergusson's grave, after he had received permission to do so from the Bailies of the Canongate Churchyard.

No sculptur'd marble here, nor pompous lay,
'No storied urn nor animated bust';
This simple stone directs pale Scotia's way,
To pour her sorrows o'er the Poet's dust.

The second line of this verse, of course, is from Gray's *Elegy*. The additional verses, not inscribed, appeared in Burns's *Second Commonplace Book*:

She mourns, sweet tuneful youth, thy hapless fate;
Tho' all the powers of song thy fancy fired,
Yet Luxury and Wealth lay by in State,
And, thankless, starv'd what they so much admired.

This humble tribute, with a tear, he gives,
A brother Bard – he can no more bestow;
But dear to fame thy Song immortal lives,
A nobler monument than Art can shew.

Epitaph on James Grieve, Laird of Boghead, Tarbolton

His estate lay west of Burns's farm of Lochlea.

Here lies Boghead amang the dead,
In hopes to get salvation;
But if such as he in Heav'n may be,
Then welcome, hail! damnation.

Epitaph on William Graham, Mossknowe

The estate of William Graham (1756–1832) lay between Annan and Ecclefechan.

'Stop thief!' Dame Nature call'd to Death,
As Willie drew his latest breath:
'How shall I make a fool again?
My choicest model thou hast ta'en.'

Epitaph for Gavin Hamilton

Gavin Hamilton (1751–1805) a lawyer, became acquainted with Burns in the autumn of 1783. At that time they were both at loggerheads with the kirk and its bigoted minister, William Auld. Hamilton was always a friend of Burns and helped him to sell many copies of his poems in the Kilmarnock Edition.

The poor man weeps – here Gavin sleeps,
Whom canting wretches blam'd;
But with such as he, where'er he be,
May I be sav'd or damn'd.

Epitaph on William Hood Senior, Tarbolton

William Hood was one of the ruling elders of the kirk that levelled its artillery against Burns for his 'immoral indiscretions'.

Here Souter Hood in death goes sleep;
To Hell, if he's gane thither,
Satan, gie him thy gear to keep;
He'll haud it weel thegither.

souter, shoemaker

Lines on the Author's Death

Written with the supposed view of being handed to John Rankine after the poet's interment.

He who of Rankine sang, lies stiff and dead,
And a green grassy hillock hides his head,
Alas, alas, a devilish change indeed.

Epitaph on Gabriel Richardson, Brewer, Dumfries

Gabriel Richardson (1759–1820) was Provost of Dumfries in 1801. The epitaph was once inscribed on a glass goblet owned by the Richardson family.

Here brewer Gabriel's fire's extinct,
And empty all his barrels:
He's blest if – as he brew'd – he drink
In upright, honest morals.

Epitaph for Captain Henderson

Captain Matthew Henderson (1737–88) was a roué and 'society' figure in Edinburgh. A man who had to sell two estates to pay for his lust for conviviality, Henderson was a 'natural' for Burns's company. On his death Burns wrote the following verses under the heading 'A gentleman who held the patent for his honours immediately from Almighty God'.

Stop, passenger! – my story's brief,
And truth I shall relate, man;
I tell nae common tale o' grief –
For Matthew was a great man.

If thou uncommon merit hast,
Yet spurn'd at Fortune's door, man,
A look of pity hither cast –
For Matthew was a poor man.

If thou a noble sodger art,
That passest by this grave, man,
There moulders here a gallant heart –
For Matthew was a brave man.

If thou on men, their works and ways,
Canst throw uncommon light, man,
Here lies wha well had won thy praise –
For Matthew was a bright man.

If thou at Friendship's sacred ca'
Wad life itself resign, man,
Thy sympathetic tear maun fa' –
For Matthew was a kind man.

If thou art staunch without a stain,
Like the unchanging blue, man,
This was a kinsman o' thy ain –
For Matthew was a true man.

25

If thou hast wit, and fun, and fire,
And ne'er gude wine did fear, man,
This was thy billie, dam, and sire –
For Matthew was a queer man.

If any whiggish whingin' sot,
To blame poor Matthew dare, man,
May dool and sorrow be his lot!
For Matthew was a rare man.

billie, companion; *queer*, amusing

Epitaph to Thomas Samson

Thomas Samson (1729–95) was a well-known seedsman in the town of Kilmarnock, Ayrshire. After a particularly good day out shooting on the moors, Samson told Burns that he would like to be buried on the moors. Burns said he would write an epitaph in readiness.

Tam Samson's weel-worn clay here lies,
Ye canting zealots, spare him!
In Honest Worth in Heaven rise,
Ye'll mend or ye wi'n near him.

'But Rab,' protested Tam, 'I'm no' deid yet!' Burns's quill scratched the vellum again.

Go, Fame, an' canter like a filly,
Thro' a' the streets an' neuks o' Killie,
Tell ev'ry social, honest billie
To cease his Grievin',
For yet unskaithed by Death's gleg gullie,
Tam Samson's livin'!

gleg gullie, sharp knife

Thomas Samson is buried in the churchyard of Laigh, Kilmarnock.

Epitaph on a Wag in Mauchline

The epitaph was to James Smith (1756–c.1823), a draper and crony of Burns. After his business failed, Smith emigrated to Jamaica.

Lament him Mauchline husband's a',
He aften did assist ye;
For had ye staid whole weeks awa',
Your wives they ne'er had miss'd ye!

Ye Mauchline bairns, as on ye pass
To school in bands thegither'
O tread ye lightly on his grass, —
Perhaps he was your faither!

Epitaph on 'Wee Johnie'

He was thought by many to be John Wilson (1759–1821), founder with his brother of the *Ayr Advertiser*, who printed Burns's first volume of poems quite unaware that Burns had written this epitaph in his honour.

Hic jacet wee Johnie
Whoe'er thou art, O reader, know,
That Death has murder'd Johnie;
An' here his *body* lies fu' low —
For *saul* he ne'er had any.

Epitaph for Mr Walter Riddell

Walter Riddell (1764–1802) was an estate owner. Burns despised him for lack of spleen.

So vile was poor Wat, sic a miscreant slave,
That the worms ev'n damn'd him when laid
    in his grave;
'In his skull there's a famine,' a starved reptile cries,
'And his heart it is poison!' another replies.

Epitaph on a Noted Coxcomb

Captain William Roddick of Corbiston

Light lay the earth on Billy's breast —
His chicken heart so tender;
But build a castle on his head,
His skull will prop it under.

Burns's Own Epitaph

Robert Burns died at his own house in Dumfries on 21 July 1796, at the age of 37. He was given a funeral with military honours and buried in a corner of St Michael's Churchyard, Dumfries. In 1815, Burns was reinterred in a specially built mausoleum, paid for out of public subscription, at a cost of around £1500.

Consigned to earth, here rests the lifeless clay,
Which once a vital spark from heaven inspired!
The lamp of genius shone full bright as day,
Then left the world to mourn its light retired.

While beams that splendid orb which lights the sphere,
While mountain streams descend to swell the main,
While changeful seasons mark the rolling years –
Thy fame, O Burns, let Scotia still retain.

A Bard's Epitaph

Burns wrote this poem as a touching 'finis' for his Kilmarnock Edition of 1786. It is unlikely that he meant it as his own epitaph, for it makes no mention of what was most dear to his heart, his wife Jean – and girls in general!

Is there a whim-inspir'd fool,
Owre fast for thought, owre hot for rule,
Owre blate to seek, owre proud to snool?
    Let him draw near;
And o'er this grassy heap sing dool.
    And drap a tear.
Is there a Bard of rustic song,
Who, noteless, steals the crowds among,
That weekly this area throng?
    O, pass not by!
But, with a frater-feeling strong.
    Here, heave a sigh.
Is there a man whose judgment clear,
Can others teach the course to steer,
Yet runs, himself, life's mad career,
    Wild as the wave?
Here pause – and thro' the starting tear,
    Survey this grave.

The poor inhabitant below
Was quick to learn and wise to know,
And keenly felt the friendly glow,
    And softer flame;
But thoughtless follies laid him low,
    And stain'd his name!
Reader attend – whether thy soul
Soars fancy's flights beyond the pole,
Or darkling grubs this earthly hole,
    In low pursuit,
Know, prudent, cautious, self-control
    Is Wisdom's root.

WHAT DID THEY DAE?

Montrose
William Fettes the Carpenter
Died 1809

The handicraft that lieth here –
For on the dead truth should appear –
Part of his bier his own hands made
And in the same his body is laid.

Deskford Churchyard, Near Cullen, Banffshire
To a Sailor Benefactor

Hic jacet Joannes Anderson, Aberdoniensis
Who built this churchard dyke at his own expences.

West Kilbride, Ayrshire
Thomas Tyre Chapman
Died 2 January 1795, aged 72.

Here lye the banes of Thomas Tyre
Wha lang had trudg'd thro' the slush and myre
In carrying bundles and sic like,
His task performing wi' small fyke;
To deal in snuff Tam aye was free,
An' served his friend for little fee;
His life obscure was nothing new,
Yet we must own his faults were few;
Although at Yule he sip'd a drap,
An' in the kirk whiles took a nap
True to his word in every case,
Tam scorned to cheat for lucre base;
Now he's gaun to taste the fare
Which none but honest men can share.

banes, bones; *myre*, mud; *sic*, such; *fyke*, trouble; *aye*,
always; *drap*, drop; *gaun*, gone.

Glasgow
Two Glasgow Politicians

Provost Aird Died *c.*1735

Here lies Provost John Aird
He was neither a great merchant, nor a great laird;
At biggin' o' kirks he had right gude skill
He was five times Lord Provost and twice
   Dean O'Guild!

Biggin' o' kirks, building churches

Bailie William Watson

Approach and read, not with your hats on
For here lies Bailie William Watson;
Who was famous for his thinking
And moderation in his drinking.

Kilmuir Cemetery, Skye
The Poor Piper

This unfinished inscription is intriguing as the payment
for its erection was never completed. The money was
to be paid by the son of the piper herein interred, but
the son 'was lost at sea in a storm while ferrying cattle
across the Minch'.

Here lye the remains of Charles Mackarter
Whose fame as an honest
Man and remarkable piper
Will survive this generation
For his manners were easy and
Regular as his music and the the
Melody of his fingers will . . .

No-one today knows of his talents or the significance of
   'the the'.

Edinburgh
A Printer's Tale

NB The puns concerning the old Scottish wood-printing-press.
Sacred to the memory of Adam Williamson Pressman-printer in Edinburgh, who died October 3, 1832; aged 72 years

All my days are loosed;
My cap is thrown off; my head is worn out;
My box is broken;
My spindle and bar have lost their power;
My till is laid aside;
Both legs of my crane are turned out of their path;
My platen can make no impression,
My winter hath no spring;
My rounce will neither roll out nor in,
Stone, coffin, and carriage have all failed;
The hinges of tympan and frisket are immovable;
My long and short ribs are rusted;
My cheeks are much worm-eaten and
    mouldering away;
My press is totally down;
The volume of my life is finished,
Not without many errors;
Most of them have arisen from bad composition,
    and are to be attributed more to the chase
    than the press;
There are also a great number of my own:
Misses, scuffs, blotches, blurs and bad register;
But the true and faithful superintendent
    has undertaken
To correct the whole.
When the machine is again set up
Incapable of decay,
A new and perfect edition of my life will appear,
Elegantly bound for duration, and every way fitted
For the grand library of the Great Author.

Durness Church, Sutherland
Vasil and vo

Donald Macmurchov hier lyis lo
Vasil to his friend var to his fo
True to his Maister, in veird and vo, 1623.

veird (weird), disaster

Mouswald, Dumfries
The Student

'In memory of J.G., Student of Physic, who perished
in the River Nith on the 22nd day of July, 1782, aged
23 years. Having attained a proficiency in Literature
and an extensive knowledge in the art of Physic, he
fell, lamented by his friends, and sincerely regretted
by all who knew him.'

Endu'd with genius and with learning stor'd,
The arduous haunts of Science he explor'd;
Fair Friendship, Truth sincere, and sense refin'd,
Blended their influence in his lib'ral mind;
Each social virtue did her powers impart,
To raise, enlarge, and harmonize his heart.
Still must his friends his fate with sorrow bear,
And sad Remembrance force the pitying tear.

Cupar, Fife
On a Fowler

Here David Forrest's corpse asleep doth lye
His soul with Christ enjoys tranquillity,
A famous fowler on the earth was he
And for the snare shall last his memory.
His years were 65 – now he doth sing
Glory to those Heavens, where
Rowth of game doth spring.

rowth, plenty

Inverness
John Stewart Died 1607

Hodie mihi cras tibi. Sic transit gloria mundi.*
Today is mine, Tomorrow yours may be
And so doth pass this world's poor pageantry.

*Literally: 'My turn today, yours tomorrow. So passes away
the glory of the world.' The latter is the German mystic monk
Thomas à Kempis's (1380–1471) comment on the transitory
nature of human vanities in *De Imitatione Christi*.

The Old Cemetery, Newport, Gwent
On Another Piper

This piper was an exile.

'To the memory of Mr John Macbeth, late piper to His
Grace the Duke of Sutherland, and a native of the
Highlands'

Died April 24th, 1852, aged 46 years

Far from his native land, beneath this stone,
Lies John Macbeth, in prime of manhood gone:
A kinder husband never yet did breathe,
A firmer friend ne'er trod on Albyn's heath!
His selfish aims were all in heart and hand,
To be an honour to his native land,
As real Scotchmen wish to fall or stand,
A handsome Gael was he of splendid form,
Fit for a siege, or for a Northern Storm.

Sir Walter Scott remarked at Inverness:
'How well becomes Macbeth the Highland dress!'
His mind was stored with ancient Highland lore,
Knew Ossian's songs, and many bards of yore;
But music was his chief, and soul's delight,
And oft he played, with Amphion's skill and might,
His Highland pipe, before our Gracious Queen!
'Mong Ladies gay, and Princesses serene!
His magic chanter's strains pur'd o'er their hearts,
With thrilling rapture soft as Cupid's darts!
Like Shakespeare's witches, scarce they drew the
    breath
But wished like them to say, 'All hail, Macbeth!'
The Queen, well pleased, gave him, by high
    command,
A splendid present from her Royal hand!
But nothing aye could make him vain or proud,
He felt alike at Court, or in a crowd;
With high and low his nature was to please,
Frank with the Peasant, with the Prince at ease.
Beloved by thousands till his race was run,
Macbeth had ne'er a foe beneath the sun;
And now he plays among the heavenly bands,
A diamond chanter never made with hands.

Biggar, Lanarkshire
The Chamberlain
Alexander Wardlaw

Chamberlain to the Rt Hon. The Earl of Wigtown.
Died 15th March 1721, aged 67 years.

Here lyes a man, whose upright heart
With virtue was profusely stor'd,
Who acted well the honest part
Between the tenants and their lord.

Betwixt the sands and flinty rock
Thus steer'd he in the golden mien;
While his blythe countenance bespoke
A mind unsullied and serene.

As to the Bruce the Fleming prov'd
Faithful, so the Fleming's heir
Wardlaw behav'd, and was belov'd
For justice, candour, faith and care.

His merit shall preserve his name
To latest ages free from rust,
Till the Archangel raise his frame
To joyn his soul amongst the just.

*Hic monumentum posuit Joannes Wardlaw,
Alexandrii filius.*

*Canongate, Edinburgh
A Musical Genius*

Epitaph for Ching Ching. A musical genius who lived
in the back streets of the city.

In silent rest beneath this green
Here sleepeth sweetly he,
Who in the body of life's scene
Was born a dwarf to be.

But who within this childlike-frame
Display'd a giant mind,
Where fires of genius high did flame,
And love of womankind!

Music to him was bread and drink,
And love the breath of life;
Of discord's jars he scorn'd to think,
And those of hate and strife.

So living, so he pass'd away,
And here his body lies;
His cherub soul, unsmudged with clay,
Soar'd up beyond the skies.

St Michael's Churchyard, Dumfries
The Wigmaker

T M Wigmaker, died 1735. M J his wife, died 1772

Two lovers true for ten years' space absented,
By stormy seas, and wars, yet liv'd contented,
We met for eighteen years, and married were.
God smil'd on us, our wind blew always fair,
We're anchor'd here waiting our Master's call,
Expecting Him, joys perpetuall.

Bedal Willy Smith

Here lyes Bedal Willy Smith,
Wha rang the auld kirk bell,
He buryed thousands in his day,
And here he lys himsel'.
Some say he was a marriyed man,
And some say he was no,
But iv he ever had a spouse,
Sh's no wi' him below.

Langholm, Dumfries
On a Drummer

'Interred here, Archibald Beattie, town drummer, who for more than half a century kept up the ancient annual custom of proclaiming the Langholm Fair at the Cross when riding the common granted to the town, and pointing out to the inhabitants thereof the various boundaries of those rights which descended from their ancestors to posterity. He died in 1823, aged 90 years. The managers of the Common-Riding for the year 1829 have caused his name to be here inscribed, as a tribute of respect justly due to his memory.'

A Teacher's Epitaph

'Charlotte Smith, who died January 17th, 1826, after having been a teacher of youth in this town for more than half a century. This stone was erected by Lieutenant (afterwards General) Pasley, of the Royal Engineers, who was her pupil in early youth.'

The Postmistress

'Margaret Easton, Postmistress, of Langholm, who died on the 24th December 1805, aged 54 years. Her virtues were uncommon. Her sorrows in life many. Erected by Charles Pasley, to the friend of his youth.'

St Michael's Churchyard, Dumfries
The Provost

To Francis Irving, Provost of Dumfries, who died in 1663

King James at first me bailie named,
Dumfries oft since me provost claimed;
God hath for me a crown reserved,
For King and Country have I served.

Langholm
The Old Soldier

'Simon Fletcher, pensioner from the 1st Royal Dragoons, in which he had served 21 years in Great Britain, Ireland, Holland, Portugal, Spain and France, where he fought in 32 battles, including Waterloo. He died February 4, 1824, aged 45 years.'

Kells Churchyard
The Merchant

Here lyeth the Corps of John McOwtie
Merchant and Burges in Newtown of Gallowie
Who departed this life feb. yie 12 1699.

Reader, wonder think it non,
Tho I cause you spike who am a ston,
Teling here of mortal dust,
And I to kipe it put in trust.

St Mungo's Churchyard, Lockerbie
The Virgin

She graced the parts of this short life
A virtuous virgin and a pleasant wife.

Bo'ness
The Hawker

If Bo'ness village you should know,
There may you hear my fyles to go,
Pins and needles, sirs, who buyes 'em,
Hard and sharp, whoever tryes 'em,
Toys and rattles, that's fit for ladyes.
Come and buy, if you'll have any
I wod fain draw the packing penny,
Whilst the pedlar thus doth bawle,
And his wares for sale doth call,
Death passes by like one unknown,
Commands him pack - His market's done.

fyles, wares

Dalnaspidal, Perthshire

In a collection of epitaphs, the epitaphologist Lady
Johnson-Ferguson noted that this was to be found
upon a stone near Scotland's highest railway station
at Dalnaspidal.

The Engine-driver

My engine now is cold and still,
No water does my boiler fill:
My coke affords it flame no more,
My days of usefulness are o'er.
My wheels deny their wonted speed,
No more my guiding hands they need;
My whistle, too, has lost its tune,
Its shrill and thrilling sounds are gone:
My valves are now thrown open wide,
My flanges all refuse to guide.
My clacks also, though once so strong,
Refuse to aid the busy throng.
No more I feel each urging breath,
My steam is now condensed in death;
Life's railway o'er, each station passed
In death I'm stopped, and rest at last.
Farewell, dear friends, and cease to weep,
In Christ I'm safe, in Christ I sleep.

Shiel, Ross and Cromarty
The Bricklayer

Silent in dust lies mouldering here
A Session Clerk of voice most clear,
None Jamie Rochus could excel
In laying bricks or singing well;
Though snapp'd his line, laid by his rod,
We build for him our hopes in God.

Symington, Lanarkshire
On a Haberdasher

Here lies John Smith, sometime Hosier and
Haberdasher in this place
He left his hose, his Anna and his love,
To sing Hosanna in the realms above.

Colintraive, Argyll
The Boozer

John Adams lies here o' the parish
A carrier who carried his ale with relish.
He carried so much, he carried so fast,
He could carry no more, so was carried at last;
For the liquor he drank being too much for one,
He could carry off so he's now carrion.

Blairingone, Clackmannanshire
Crummy Abercrombie of the Penny Whistle

Here Crummy lies, enclosed in wood,
Full six feet one and better,
When tyrant Death grim o'er him stood,
He faced him like a hatter.

Now he lies low without a boot,
Free from this world of bustle,
And silent now is Crummy's flute,
And awfie dry his whustle.

Arbroath
The Treasurer

Here lyes Alexander Peter, who died 12 January 1630
Such a Treasurer was not since, nor yet before,
For common work
Calsais, Brigs and shoir,
Of all others he did escel;
He devised our school and he hung our bell.

calsais, causeways; *brigs*, bridges; *schoir*, sewers

Kinnoull, Perthshire
The Flautist

Halt for a moment,
Passenger and read,
Here Andrew dozes
In his daisied bed.

Silent his flute
Torn off its key,
His genius scattered
And the Muse set free.

Wigtown Churchyard
A Smalltime Shopkeeper

Here lies John Taggart, of honest fame,
Of stature low, and a leg lame;
Content he was with portion small,
Kept a shop in Wigtown, and that's all.

Kirkmichael Churchyard, Banffshire

In memory of J A Mason who lost his life suddenly after a fall.

How necessary it is to be,
Prepared for death – pray learn from me.

The Innkeeper
R.B. late innkeeper of Dumfries

To Mother Earth dissolv'd we lie
But naught of us but what could die.

Hoddom Churchyard, Dumfries

To the Revd Matthew Reid, died 1680

His name he from St Matthew took,
His skill in physic from St Luke:
A reed of John the Baptist's kind,
Not wandering with every wind;
Ever a true Nathaniel,
He lived, preached, and died well.

Applegarth Churchyard, Dumfries
On a Cattle Thief

Beneath this stone lies Peter White
For all the ills he got the wight,
For stealing sheep, and kye and corn,
The like of him was never known.

got the wight, was made responsible

West Longrigg, Lanarkshire
He broke all existing records

Erected in grateful remembrance of Thomas Wishart, who died 1752, aged 125 years.

His record was beaten, however, for in the graveyard at Leadhills, Lanarkshire, is the gravestone of John Taylor who is reputed to have died in 1770, aged 137 years.

Melrose Abbey, Roxburghshire

In the west wall of the south transept of St Mary's ruined Cistercian Abbey at Melrose is this plaque set as a posthumous testimony to a French master-mason who worked on the abbey, as well as on ecclesiastical sites including the cathedrals of Glasgow and St Andrews and Paisley Abbey:

John Morrow sum tym callit was I,
And born in Parysse certanly,
And had in kepyng and mason work
Of Santandroys ye hye kirk
Of Glasgo, Melros, and Paslay
Of Nyddysdall and of Galway
I pray to God, Mari bathe
& swete Sanct Johne, to kepe
This haly kirk fra skathe.

Graveyard, Jedburgh Abbey, Roxburghshire
A Cautionary Wish

Here lies T. Winter Architect
And late Baielie of Jedburgh
Who died the 17 September
1730 Aged 61 years and who
himself ordered this
Inscription

Whosoever Removes This
Stone
Or Causes it to be Removed
May he die the last of
All his Friends.

The churchyard of the Grey Friars, Perth
John Conqueror, bailie of Perth, died 1653

O'er death a conqueror here lies whose soul
Freed from the dust triumphs above the pole;
One less than twice twelve children by one wife
He had, of whom, to everlasting life
Twice ten he sent before him, and behind
He left but three to propagate his kind;
He ran ten lustres out when rigid fate
Robbed him of life and Perth a Magistrate.

Banchory, N Kincardineshire

John Gray, Messenger-at-Arms, died 1806,
wrote this himself:

Poor John Gray! Here he lies,
Nobody laughs and nobody cries;
Where he's gone, and how he fares,
Nobody knows and nobody cares.

Gordon
The Tall Schoolmaster

Ah, he was great in body and in mind
A loving husband and a father kind.
As he most men exceded in his stature,
So he exceled in his literature.
But although he is gone and greatly mist
God's will be done, we hope he is blest.

PAWKY WISDOM

Haddington
About Marion Gray

If modesty commend a wife,
And providence a mother,
Grave chastity a widow's life
We'll not find such an other
In Haddington as Marion Gray.
Who here doth lie till the doomsday
She was deceased 29 December 1655
And her age was 60.

Dunkeld, Perth

On Margery Scott, who lived single 25 years, married
25 years and widowed 50 years.

Stop, reader, here until my life you've read,
The living may gain knowledge from the dead:
Five times five years I was a married wife;
Ten times five years a widow grave and chaste;
Now, wearied of this mortal life, I rest.
I from my cradle to my grave have seen
Eight mighty kings of Scotland and a queen;
Four times five years the Commonwealth I saw,
Ten times the subjects rise against the law;
Twice did I see old prelacy put down,
And twice the cloak did sink beneath the gown;
An end of Stuart's race I saw — nay more
I saw my country sold for English gold
Such desolation in my life have seen
That I've an end of all perfection seen.

The Necropolis, Glasgow

Stranger as you pass o'er this grass;
Think seriously, with no humdrumming,
Prepare for death, for judgement's coming.

45

Eskdalemuir, Dumfries
Average John

Here lies JOHN LAURIE
Neither rich nor poor,
Last minister of Wauchope,
And first of Eskdalemuir.

Montrose
Backlog

Here lyes the bodyes of George Young and
Isabel Guthrie, and all their posteritie for
fifty years backwards. NOV 1757

Inverness
Pay Attention Reader

Ask thou, who lies within the place so narrow?
I'm here today, thou may'st be here to-morrow;
Dust must return to dust, our mother;
The soul returns to God the Father.

On the stone set up for a glover, died 1687

This world is a citie
Full of streets
Death Ye mercat
That a' men meets
If life were a thing
That monie cold buy
The piur cold not not live
And ye rich wold not die.

Kilmahog

A septuagenarian's advice, 1700

Weep not for me who here do lye,
Weep for your sins before you dye;
For death is not to lamented
But sin is still to be repented.

46

Melrose
Wisdom from the Abbey

The earth goeth on the earth,
Glistening like gold,
The earth goes to the earth,
Sooner than it wold.
The earth builds on the earth
Castles and towers;
The earth says to the earth,
All shall be ours.

St Michael's Churchyard, Dumfries

In memory of J M, died 31 August 1708, aged 50.

If grace, good manners, gifts of mind,
Yea where all moral virtues have combined,
Compleat a man, behold beneath this stone,
Here lyes interred, whom rich and poor bemoan,
He ran his race, abundant entrance got,
His name is savori, and shall not rot.

savori, possessing unction

Granton, Edinburgh

My death came sudden it was my lot
To be killed dead upon the spot
Alas dear friends for me don't mourn
I'm gone where travellers ne'er return.

Kind angels saw the blooming girls
Whose only virtue crowned their joy,
And out of their excess of love,
They snatched them to themselves above.

Sharp was the stroke that did appear
To take his life away;
O Reader then, for Heaven prepare
On earth you cannot stay.

Elgin Cathedral

Censure not rashly,
Though nature's apt to halt,
No woman's born,
That dies without a fault.

47

The Howff, Dundee
On Mr Speid

Time flies with speed; with speed Speid's fled
To the darkest regions of the dead,
With speed consumption's sorrows flew
And stopped Speid's speed, for Speid it slew.
Miss Speid beheld with frantic woe
Poor Speid with speed turn pale as snow,
And beat her chest and tore her hair,
For Speid, poor Speid, was all her care.
Let's learn from Speid with speed to fly
From sin, since we like Speid, must die.

Two from Glasgow
Mr Ball the Baker

Here I lie – my name is Ball –
I lived – I died, despised by all:
And now I cannot chew my crust;
I'm going back to my ancient dust.

Stop, reader! I have left a world
In which there was a world to do;
Fretting and stewing to be rich
Just such a fool as you.

Kirkmichael Churchyard
To Revd Mr John Allan, died 1752

This modest stone, which few vain marbles can,
May justly say, here lies an Honest Man.

Inverkip, Renfrewshire
John So, Tailor

Here lies John So
So so did he so
So did he live
So did he die
So so did he so
So let him lye.

Trailflat Churchyard

Thomas C died Sept 1763, aged 23;
William C died Sept 1763

Think not, young men,
On threescore ten,
Or yet of long fourscore,
But quite the stage,
At any age,
As these have done before.

In memory of B C, died December 1801, aged 64

'On what a slender thread hangs Everlasting things'.

Mouswald Churchyard

In memory of A Bell, Schoolmaster of Mouswald,
Who died Jan 8th MDCCXCIII, aged 31 years.

Honourable age is not that which standeth in length
Of Time,
Nor that is measured by number of years.
But wisdom is the gray hair unto men,
And unspotted life is old age.

Langbank, Renfrewshire
To John McVitie, 1669

Feare God, dear friends, dry tears away,
For he that deyath in Christ he lives for aye
Remember death when you view this stone,
Sigh passenger, and so you will be
    when you're gone.

Who eire thou be that do comy by,
Know John McVitie hier doth lye;
Intered sure under this stone
By Gavin McVitie, his eldest sone.

J R 1715

For dust from dust at first was taken;
Tho dust by dust be now forsaken
Yet dust on dust must still remain;
Till dust return to dust again.
Pray, reader, as thou goest by,
Think on thine own mortality:
Remember well that die thou must;
And lie as I do in the dust.

Fife

HIC JACET
1 . . . 5 − 4

0 . . . 4 . . . 1 . . . 2 . . . 8
0 . . . 4 . . . 1 . . . 2 . . . 0
0 . . . 2 . . . 80 . . . 8
0 . . . 2 . . . 45 . . . 4

Morton, Dumfries

Janet Johnstoun relek to William Armstrong
wha sett uppe thys monument
anno domo 1660
Man is grass, to grave he flies,
Grass decays and man he dies
Grass revives, and man does rise,
Yet few then appreciated the prise.

Colvend

Advice from J L 1825

I' youth prepare thyself to die,
For life is short, and death is nigh,
Death did me little warning give,
Therefore be careful how you live.

O, Death thou dids't no pity show,
For thou hast laid my wife full low,
And left me here alone to mourne
A widower sad from even to morn.

My sorrows I will moderate,
I will not weep but meditate,
The pleasing hope I'll entertain,
That we in joy shall meet again.

St Mungo's Churchyard, Lockerbie
On a stone with two figures each side of an apple tree.

Here stands Adam and Eve, tree and all,
Whereby whose fall
We were made sinners all.

Trailflat
Memento Morte. M B

Stop, Passenger, when this you view,
Remember I was once like you,
A feeble worm, a clod of earth;
Man's life is death, e'en from his birth.

This is perhaps Scotland's most common epitaph sentiment. Here's another version from St Fillans, Forgan, Fife, dated 1793:

See passenger as you pass by
As ye are now so once was I
As I am now so must you be
Remember man that thou must die.

Church of the Holy Rude, Stirling

On Alex E Meffen, Chief Constable of Stirlingshire.
He served in Stirling (1858–64).

Our life is but a winter day;
Some only breakfast and away;
Others to dinner stay
And are full fed:
The oldest man but sups
And goes to bed.
Large is his debt
That lingers out the day;
He that goes soonest
Has the least to pay.

Garrel Churchyard, Dumfries
John Henry, Surgeon, 1798

A serious friend may drop a tear
On these dear bones and say
These once were strong as mine appear,
And mine must be as they.

Minnigaff
Agnes Douglas, 1777

This Grave is but a finning pot,
Unto Believers arise, for when the
Soul hath lost its dross, it like the
Son shall rise.

finning, refining

Luce Churchyard, Hoddom Parish

Here lyes ane honest Gentleman
called Adam Carlel of Milflet, 1681
His age 96.
The youngest may die but
The aged must,
Sooner or later return
to dust.

Kirkmahoe Churchyard
R G who was killed by an overturning cart, 1818

Here lieyes within this narrow vale
A youth who in a moment fell,
And by the hand of violent death
Resigned to heaven his fleeting breath.

Kells Churchyard
Jean Sloan, died 6 October, 1732

Death's steps
    are swift,
And yet no nois
    maks
His hands unseen,
    and yet
Most shurely
    taks.

Kelton

Our sons they sleep down in this grave,
We will not weep to wake them;
We will wait till death do come,
And we will overtake them.

Anwoth, Kirkcudbrightshire
M M, died 1612

Walking with God, in puritie of life,
In Christ I died and endit al my strife,
For in my saule Christ did here dwell by grace,
Now dwells my saule in glory of his face,
Therefoir my bodie sal not hier remaine
But to ful glory quicklie rise againe.

Luss Churchyard, Dumbartonshire

Could he disclose, who rests below
The things beyond the grave that lie,
We more should learn than now we know,
But know no better how to die.

SAFE FRAE THE WIFE

Churchyard of Alves, Morayshire

Here lies 1590
ANDERSON OF PITTENSERE
haire of the earldom of Moray
with his wife MARJORY
whilk him never displicit

Balone, Fife

Of children in all she bore him twenty four:
Thank the Lord there will be no more.

Potterhill, Paisley

Here lies Mary, the wife of John Ford,
We hope her soul is gone to the Lord;
But if for Hell she has chang'd this life
She had better be there than be John Ford's wife.

Cambuskenneth Abbey

Burial place of James III and his Queen

HERE LIES THE BODY OF JAMES ROBERTSON
AND RUTH HIS WIFE
'Their warfare is accomplished'

Devonside, Clackmannanshire

Here lies my poor wife,
A sad slattern and shrew.
If I said I regretted it,
I should lie too.

Kelso Abbey
John Dunn 1653

Should I fear death,
That ends my seed,
And worldly cares cutts aff me?
Should I crave life,
With strut and strife
And Satan still to chaff me?
No; welcome death;
Come forth, poor breath!
Thou hast too long been thrall
O Trinity in Unity,
Rescue my silly soul
And the wife too.

Prestonpans Churchyard

WILLIAM MATTHISON here lies
Whose age was forty-one;
February 17 he dies
Went Isbel Mitchell from;
Who was his married wife,
The fourth part of her life.

The soul it cannot die
Though the body be turned to clay,
Yet meet again they must
At the last day.
Trumpet shall sound, archangels cry:
'Come forth, Isbel Mitchell, and meet Will
Matthison in the sky'.

Kirkmahoe Churchyard

Under this stone lo, here doth ly
A woman who was miserly.
Her husband she ran a race to Hell
And now she has gone there hersel'.

And

Rest in peace my wife Chatt Beck
Who rode to hounds and broke her neck.

Greyfriars Kirkyard, Edinburgh

Here snug in a grave my wife doth lie,
She is at rest, and so am I,
Who for beneath this stone doth rest
Has joined the army of the blest.
The lord has taken her to the sky;
The Saints rejoice, and so do I
Tears cannot restore her, therefore I cry.

Invermallie, Inverness

Here lyeth wrapped in clay
The body of Ester Wray:
I have no more to say
Except bless the day
She went away
3rd May
1872.

Lunan Churchyard

Epitaph composed by Revd Henry Ogilvy.

Here lies the smith, to wit Tom Gowk,
His father and his mither,
Wi' Dick, and Neil, and Meg and Jock,
And a' the Gowks thegither.
When on the yird, my wife and I
'Greed desperate ill wi' ither;
But here, withoutten strife or din
We tak' a nap thegither.

Colvend, Kirkcudbrightshire
A coo, a pig and a wife

Collected by Revd James Mackeachie at Colvend.

Jock Tamson haed a coo,
Jock Tamson haed a pig,
Jock Tamson haed a nyatterin wife
That play't him monie a rigg.
Jock Tamson's sleepin' soun
I' the Col'stone caul' Kirkyard —
An' Meg has met 'er marrow
She's coupl't wi'a Kyard.

rigg, trick; *marrow*, match; *kyard*, tinker

6

SOME FAMOUS FOLK

Calton Hill, Edinburgh
David Hume (1711–76) the celebrated historian and philosopher

Within this circular idea
Called vulgarly a tomb,
The ideas and impressions lie
That constituted Hume.

From Sweetheart Abbey, Dumfriesshire

Composed by Hugh de Burgh, Prior of Lanercost, on Devorgilla, who died in 1289, the widow of John Baliol.

In Devorvilla moritur sensata Sibilla
Cum Marthaque pia, contemplativa Maria
Da Devorvillam requie, Rex summe potiri
Quam tegit iste lapis cor pariterque viri

In Devorgilla, a sybil doth die, as
Mary Contemplative, as Martha pious;
To her, Oh! deign, high King, rest to impart
Whom this stone covers with her husband's heart.

Balquhidder, Perthshire, near Rob Roy's grave

Beneath this stane lies Shanet Roy,
Shon Roy's reputed mother;
In all her life this Shon Roy
She never had another.

'Tis here or hereabouts, they say,
The place no one can tell;
But when she'll rise at the last day,
She'll ken the stane hersel'.

Island of Juan Fernandez
In memory of Alexander Selkirk, Mariner

A native of Largo, in the county of Fife, Scotland.
Who lived on this island, in complete solitude,
for four years and four months.
He was landed from the 'Cinque Ports' galley,
96 tons, 18 guns, AD 1704, and
was taken off in the 'Duke', Privateer,
12th February 1709.
He died Lieutenant of HMS 'Weymouth'
AD 1723, aged 47.
This tablet is erected near Selkirk's lookout
By Commander Powell and the officers
of HMS 'Topaze', AD 1868.

Selkirk was the inspiration for *Robinson Crusoe* by Daniel Defoe.

At ruined Kailzie church, Peeblesshire

Gulielmus Horsburgh
De eodem obiit.
Edinburg Septimo
Julii, 1711 anno
Aetat xxiv.

Of four and twenty years of age here lies
The apparent chief of two old families.
The Horsburgh of that Ilk, and Tait of Pirn,
Lies in one person in his isle and urn;
A man of courage, strength and comely feature,
Of a good temper and oblidging nature.

The Horsburghs of that Ilk, of Pirn House, were a prominent Border family. During his tour of the Borders in 1787, Robert Burns took tea with the family at their home on the Gala Water. The house has long since been demolished and the Horsburghs died out in the male line in 1911.

The Poet James Thomson

In memory of James Thomson

Others to marble may their glory owe,
And boast those honours sculpture can bestow;
Short lived renown; that every moment must
Sink with its emblem and consume to dust
But Thomson needs no artist to engrave
From dumb oblivion no device to save.
Such vulgar aids let names inferior ask,
Nature for him assumes herself a task;
THE SEASONS are his monuments of fame,
With them they flourish, as from them they came.

Born at Ednam, Roxburghshire, 1700. Died 1748. His
poem *The Seasons* appeared as a set in 1730.

From Fogo, Berwickshire

Here lyes the body and the banes
Of the mighty Laird of Whinkerstanes
He had nae other God ava'
But Rosiebank and Charterha'.

Rosiebank and Charterhall were two large local estates.

The prominent Provost of Perth

Colin Brown, a provost of Perth who became a legend
in his own lifetime, had this epitaph written for him by
his friend Ralph Erskine of Dunfermline, who was the
author of *Gospel Sonnets*:

Friend, do not, careless on thy road,
O'erlook this humble shrine,
For if thou art a friend of God,
Here ly's a friend of thine.

His closet was a Bethel sweet,
His house a house of prayer.
In homely strain at Jesus' feet,
He daily wrestled there.

He to the City was a guide,
And to the Church a fence;
Nor could within the camp abide
When truth was banish'd thence.

His life and death did both express,
What strength of grace was given.
His life a lamp of holiness,
His death a dawn of heaven.
VIVE MEMOR LETHI: FUGIT HORA.

The Latin tag used in the epitaph means: 'Live mindful of death: time flies', and was written by the first-century AD Roman poet Persius. The quote is incomplete and should go on, *hoc quod loquor inde est* – 'this very word I speak is so much taken from it'.

The Wealthy Beggar

Some folk were celebrated in their own area for being 'characters'. One such was William Kerr from Montrose who died in 1772.

To the Memory of WILLIAM KERR
Not more remarkable for the lowness of his Stature
Than for the Integrity of his Life
Tho' he acquired great Wealth
He never abused it,
For
He was neither a Spendthrift nor an Usurer
He lent freely,
But seldom exacted Interest, or Principal.
He was always ready to minister to the Stranger,
Not only with his Services, but also with his
Prayers.
Tho' generally an Attendant at Taverns,
He ever waited at Church,
And was so assiduous in Business,
That he never lost an Hour in Dissipation.
Luxury and Riot were no otherwise known to him,
Than what he saw in other Men,
And he improved thereby.
Reader
These lines are guiltless of Flattery
For he
To whose Memory they are wrote,
Was neither a Lord, nor a Squire,
But a Beggar.

King Robert I, The Bruce

Robert I (1306–29), son of Robert Bruce, Earl of Carrick and Annandale, and Marjorie, Countess of Carrick, ascended the throne of Scotland when he was 31 and died when he was 54 at Cardross, Dumbarton. On his deathbed he asked that his heart be removed from his body, embalmed and carried to the Holy Sepulchre at Jerusalem; Bruce had always wanted to go on a holy crusade to the Holy Land. So, bearing Bruce's heart, Sir James Douglas went into battle with the Moors. In due time Bruce's heart was brought back to Scotland and interred in St Mary's Abbey at Melrose. Probably it would have been placed before the high altar at the abbey. However, during excavations in the chapter-house in 1921 a mummified human heart was found enclosed in a cone-shaped container of lead, and decomposed iron box straps around it showed that it had once been placed in a coffer. Some scholars are tempted to aver that this was Bruce's heart placed in the chapter-house to avoid despoilation at the Reformation.

The body of Robert Bruce was taken from Cardross to Dunfermline and laid in a grave in the middle of the choir of the abbey church. Above the king's body a French 'fair tomb' of white marble was erected with this epitaph:

HIC JACET INVICTUS ROBERTUS, REX BENEDICTUS
QUI SUA GESTA LEGIT REPETAT QUOT BELLA PEREGIT
AD LIBERTATEM PERDUXIT PER PROBITATEM
REGNUM SCOTORUM: NUNC VIVAT IN ARCE POLORUM.

('Here lies the unconquered and blessed King Robert. Whosoever collects together [*the records of*] his warlike deeds, may recount what wars he prosecuted. He led the Kingdom of the Scots through uprightness to liberty; now he lives in the Citadel of Heaven.')

At the Reformation, part of the buildings of Dunfermline Abbey were demolished and for centuries the site of Bruce's tomb was lost. Finally, when the site was being cleared in 1818 for the erection of the new abbey church, the tomb was rediscovered with Bruce's skeleton – with severed breastbone showing where the heart had been extracted – wrapped in cloth of gold. The king was reburied and in 1889 the Earl of Elgin gifted a memorial brass to cover the grave, set in a base of Italian porphyry, with:

ROBERTI DE BRVS SCOTORVM REGIS SEPVLCHRVM.
AD MDCCCXVIII INTER RVINAS PAVSTE RETECTVM HOC AERE
DENVO CONSIGNATVM EST ANNO POST IPSIVS OBITVM DLX.

'The tomb of Robert Bruce, King of Scots, fortunately discovered among the ruins in 1818, has been marked anew by this brass in the 560th year after his death.'

Rothesay Churchyard
On two French exiles

STEPHANIE-HORTENSE-MARIE
MATILDE-ELIZABETH-AMELIE-
BONAPARTE. MORTE LE 1 JUILLET
1885
JE SAIS QUE MON REDEMTEUR EST
VIVANT,
ET QU'IL DEMEURERA LE DERNIER
SUR LA TERRE,
ET QU'APRE QUE MA PEAU, AURA
ETE
DETRUITE,
JE VERRAI DIE DE MA CHAIR,
JE LE VERRAI MOI MEME,
ET MES YEUX LE VERRONT,
ET NON UN AUTRE.
WIFE OF
BENJAMIN ST JOHN BAPTISTE JOULE,
BORN 8/11/1817.
DIED AT 36 MOUNT STUART RD.
21/5/1895.

The inscription *Je sais que mon redemteur est vivant* (I know that my Redeemer lives) comes from Job 19:25-26, and the whole text is in imperfect French.

The Grave with the Curse

In the churchyard at Rothiemurchus, near Aviemore, is a grave known locally as 'The Grave with the Curse'. The burial ground is celebrated as the last resting-place of the local lairds. One such laird was Farquhar Shaw who defeated the Davidsons of Invernahaven in battle in 1396. On his grave are five cylindrical stones of granite, and the local old wives' tale recounts that anyone removing these stones is rewarded by sudden death. Nearby is the tombstone of one who did just that, and paid the price!

In 1856, 22-year-old Robert Scroggie, a footman to Elizabeth, Duchess of Bedford (Francis, 9th Duke of Bedford had the tenancy of nearby Doune House), removed one of the stones as a joke. He was drowned whilst bathing in the Spey a few days later!

The local stories do note that the Shaw stones once came from a burial mound a short distance away . . . a mound guarded by a 'Brownie', a particularly mischievous spirit of Scottish elflore.

A Prankster at Kells

On John Murray's grave – he was a gamekeeper at Kenmure estate and is buried at Kells, Kirkcudbrightshire – is a curious stone showing a fishing rod, a gun, a powder flask and, back-to-back, a pheasant and a gun dog. Murray died in 1777 and the local parish minister, the Revd Gillespie, wrote this to be inscribed at the back of the headstone:

Ah, John what changes since I saw thee last;
Thy fishing and thy shooting days are past.
Bagpipes and hautboys thou canst sound no more;
Thy nods, grimaces, winks, and pranks are o'er.
Thy harmless, queeirsh, incoherent talk,
Thy wild vivacity, and trudging walk,
Will be quite forgot, thy joys on earth –
A snuff, a glass, riddles, and noisy mirth –
Are vanished all. Yet blest, I hope, thou art,
For, in thy station, well thou playdst thy part.

The murderers of Magus Muir

On 3 May 1679, James Sharp, the episcopal Archbishop of St Andrews, was returning to St Andrews with his daughter Isabel when their coach was waylaid by a band of assassins at Magus Muir, near to the village of Strathkinness, Fife. Once the Presbyterian minister of Crail, Sharp had been Professor of Theology at St Andrews and had thrown in his lot with the Royalist Revolutionaries, one of the two factions into which the Scottish Covenanters divided themselves. The Covenanters was the name given to the signatories of the Scottish National Covenant in 1638 who were pledged to uphold the Presbyterian faith against prelacy and popery. The national feeling aroused led to the Bishops' Wars of 1639 and 1640 wherein resistance was stirred up against the arbitrary rule of Charles I, when in 1637, with the aid of Archbishop Laud, he tried to enforce the use of the English liturgy in Scotland.

To those who adhered strictly to the Covenant, James Sharp was an anathema and was blamed, quite unjustly, for many of the unpopular measures which were dictated by the Privy Council. So Sharp was a marked man and at Magus Muir he was dragged from his coach and hacked to death by nine Presbyterian fanatics in front of his daughter. In fact Sharp was murdered by mistake; the killers were hunting for William Carmichael, sheriff-substitute of Fife and a well-known persecutor of Presbyterians, when Sharp passed by.

Today, a memorial pyramid of stones from the sea marks the spot at Magus Muir where Sharp was murdered. But his Dutch-work white and black marble tomb is to be found in Holy Trinity Church, St Andrews. On the tomb's pedestal is a representation of the murder scene. The epitaph, one of the most effusive in Scotland, was written by Andrew Bruce, Bishop of Dunkeld:

D[OMINO] O[PTIMO] M[AXIMO] SACRATISSIMI ANTISTITIS PRUDENT-ISSIMI SENATORIS SANCTISSIMI MARTYRIS CINERES PRECIOS-ISSIMOS / SUBLIME HOC TEGIT MAUSOLEUM / HIC NAMQ[UE] JACET / QUOD SUB SOLE RELIQUUM EST REVERENDISSIMI IN XTO PATRIS / D.D. JACOBI SHARP S[ANC]TI ANDREÆ ARCHI : EPISCOPI TOTIUS SCOTIÆ PRIMATIS &C / QUEM / PHILOSOPHIÆ ET THEOLOGIÆ PROFESSOREM ACA- DEMIA PRESBYTERUM DOCTOREM PRÆSULEM ECCLESIA / TUM ECCLESIASTICI TUM CIVILIS STATUS MINISTRUM PRIMARIUM SCOTIA / SERENISSIMI *CAROLI* SECUNDI MONARCHICIQ[UE] IMPERII RESTITUTIONIS SUASOREM BRITANNIA / EPISCOPALIS ORDINIS IN SCOTIA INSTAURATOREM CHRISTIANUS ORBIS / PIETA[T]IS EXEMPLUM PACIS ANGELUM SAPIENTIÆ ORACULUM GRAVITATIS IMAGINEM BONI ET FIDELES SUBDITI / IMPIETATIS PERDUELLIONIS ET SCHISMATIS HOSTEM ACERRIMUM / DEI REGIS ET GREGIS INIMICI VIDERUNT AGNOVERUNT ADMIRABANTUR / QUEMQ[UE] TALIS ET TANTUS CUM ESSET NOVEM CONJURATI PARRICIDÆ FANATICO FURORE PERCITI / IN METROPOLITICÆ SUÆ CIVITATIS VICINIO LUCENTE MERIDIANO SOLE CHARISSIMA FILIA / PRIMOGENITA ET DOMESTICIS FAMULIS VULNERATIS LACHRIMANTIBUS RECLAMANTIBUS / IN GENUA UT PRO IPSIS ETIAM ORARET PROLAPSUM QUAMPLURIMIS VULNERIBUS /

CONFOSSUM SCLOPETIS GLADIIS PUGIONIBUS HOR[R]ENDUM
IN MODUM TRUCIDARUNT / 3º DIE MAIJ J6 79
ÆTATIS SUÆ 61

('To the Glory of God. This lofty tomb covers the
unspeakably precious dust of the holiest of bishops,
the sagest of state-councillors, the most saintly of mar-
tyrs, for here lies all that remains beneath the sun
of the Most Reverend Father in Christ, James Sharp,
Doctor of Divinity, Archbishop of St Andrews, Primate
of all Scotland, etc., whom the University regarded,
acknowledged and continually marvelled at as a professor of theology and philosophy, the Church as priest,
teacher, and leader, Scotland as its Prime Minister,
ecclesiastical and lay, Britain as the advocate of the
restoration of His Most Gracious Majesty, Charles the
Second, and of the monarchy, the world of Christianity
as the man who re-established the order of Episcopacy
in Scotland, good and faithful subjects as a model of
piety, an angel of peace, an oracle of wisdom and a pic-
ture of dignity, enemies of God, the King, and the people as the bitterest foe of irreligion, treason and schism,
and whom despite his character and eminence nine
sworn assassins, inspired by fanatical rage, did with
pistols, swords and daggers most foully massacre close
to his metropolitan seat, under the noonday sun, with
his beloved eldest daughter and his personal attendants
bleeding, weeping and protesting, on May 3rd, 1679, in
the sixty-first year of his age, piercing him with countless
wounds when he had fallen on his knees to pray even
for his murderers.')

Five Covenanters — Thomas Brown, James Wood, Andrew Sword, John Waddell and John Clyde — were taken prisoner at the Battle of Bothwell Bridge (where the Covenanters were defeated by the Duke of Monmouth), and despite having nothing to do with Sharp's murder, were hanged in chains on 25 November 1679. Their monument lies in an open field near to Sharp's pyramid and was set up in 1877 by the local landowner John Whyte-Melville:

'Cause we at Bothwell did appear,
Perjurious oaths refuse to swear:
'Cause we Christ's cause would not condemn
We were sentenced to death by men
Who raged against us in such fury,
Our dead bodies they did not bury,
But up on poles did hang us high,
Triumphs of Babel's victory.
Our lives we feared not to the death,
But constant proved to our last breath.

Also restored in 1877 was the memorial to one Andrew Guillan who had been present at Sharp's murder. Tradition has it that he played no active part in the murder but in due time he was arrested, tried and hanged at Edinburgh and his cadaver suspended in chains by the stream not far from modern Claremont farm south of Strathkinness. Above his grave a monument was set up in 1783:

A faithful martyr here doth lie,
A witness against perjurie,
Who cruelly was put to death
To gratify proud prelates' wrath;
They cut his hands ere he was dead,
And after that struck off his head;
To Magus Muir they did him bring,
His body on a pole did hing;
His blood under the altar cries
For vengeance on Christ's enemies.

A famous Scott original

At the old burial ground of Roxburgh, Roxburghshire, this stone was once purported to be seen:

The Body of the
Gentleman Beggar
Andrew Gemmels, alias Edie
Ochiltree, was interred here,
Who died at Roxburgh Newton
In 1793
Aged 106 years.
Erected by William Thomson, Farmer,
Over Roxburgh
1849.

Andrew Gemmels featured in Walter Scott's *Antiquary* as Edie Ochiltree a 'king's bedesman' (a pauper enjoying royal bounty), a travelling beggar whose easy manner put him on terms of familiarity with high and low.

Epitaphs to the Stuarts

There are no more emotive epitaphs that those to the Stuarts in St Peter's basilica in Rome. On the coffins of Charles Edward Stuart – the Jacobite Charles III, and his brother Cardinal Henry Benedict, Duke of York – the Jacobite Henry IX, who actually died in 1807, are these epitaphs:

D.O.M.
CAROLUS III
JACOBI III FILIUS
MAGNÆ BRITAN
FRANC: ET HIBER.R
NATUS MDCCXX
OB. PRID.KAL.FEBR
M.D.CCLXXXVIII.

'To the Lord God, supreme ruler of the world. Charles III, son of James III, King of Great Britain, France and Ireland, born 1720: died February 1788.'

In reality Charles died on 31 January: Lord Stanhope often told the story that Charles died on 30 January, but that the news had been suppressed as that was the anniversary of the execution of Charles I, a sorry day in Stuart lore.

D.O.M.
HENRICUS IX
JACOBI III FILIUS
MAGNA BRIT: FRANC: ET HIBER R
DUX EBORACENSIS NUNCUPATUS
EPUS: OSTIEND. ET VELITER
S.R.E. VICE CANCELLAR: S.C.DECANUS
BASILICAE VATICAN; ARCHPR
TUSCULI SANCTISSIME
OBIIT DIE XIII JUL: ANNI 1707 [*sic*]
VIXIT ANN. LXXXII. M.IV.D.VII.

'To the Lord God, supreme ruler of the world. Henry
IX, son of James III, King of Great Britain, France and
Ireland, self-styled Duke of York, Bishop of Ostia and
Vellatri, Vice-Chancellor of the Holy Roman Church,
Dean of the Sacred College, Archpriest of the Vatican
Basilica, died in the odour of sanctity on July 13th,
1707, aged 82 years, 4 months and 7 days.'

Over the tombs of the Stuart princes, George IV – or,
it is averred by some, Pope Pius VIII, helped by a
donation of fifty guineas (£51.05) from George IV –
raised the famous white marble monument by Antonio
Canova with the inscription:

JACOBO III
JACOBI.II.MAGNAE.BRIT.REGIS.FILIO
KAROLO. EDUARDO
ET. HENRICO, DECANO. PATRUM. CARDINALIUM
JACOBI.III.FILIIS
REGIAE. STIRPIS. STVARDIAE. POSTREMIS
ANNO M.D.CCC.XIX.

BEATE MORTUI QUI IN DOMINO MORIUNTUR.

'James III, son of James II,
King of Great Britain, Charles Edward
and Henry, Dean of the Cardinals
sons of James III, last of the
royal House of Stuart, 1819'.

'Blessed are they who die in the Lord'.

Fernie Castle Hotel, Fife
A celebrated canine

There are very few epitaphs extant in Scotland to animals, so the touching tribute to an old dog at Fernie Castle Hotel, Fife, is doubly interesting. Set into the hearth of the hotel's barrel-vaulted bar is the epitaph:

Busdubh, 1904-1921.
This is my humble prayer,
Nor may I pray in vain,
God make me good enough
To meet my dog again.

The story goes that the dog belonged to the Balfour family who once owned the castle. The black labrador, called Busdubh, was a faithful family pet who was buried under the cellar floor of the castle. When the castle was converted into a hotel the epitaph was set in a wall, but later it was moved and set into the hearthstone of the bar . . . only a few feet away from where the dog is buried.